reincarnation

reincarnation

KRYS & JASS GODLY

Previously published in 2010 as *Simply Reincarnation* by
Zambezi Publishing Limited, Devon, UK

This edition first published in Great Britain in 2017 by
Orion
an imprint of the Orion Publishing Group Ltd
Carmelite House, 50 Victoria Embankment,
London, EC4Y 0DZ
An Hachette UK Company

*Although this book discusses past-life regression as a therapy, it is important that if
you have any history of mental health challenges, you seek professional advice before
trying to put yourself into any kind of altered state.*

*All example stories in this book have been used with the permission of the client, and
names have been changed to protect identities.*

1 3 5 7 9 10 8 6 4 2

Interior design by Kathryn Sky-Peck

A CIP catalogue record for this book is available
from the British Library.

Paperback ISBN: 978 1 4091 6977 2

eBook ISBN: 978 1 4091 6978 9

Printed and bound by CPI Group (UK), Ltd, Croydon, CR0 4YY

MIX
Paper from
responsible sources
FSC® C104740

www.orionbooks.co.uk

We dedicate this book to our
wonderful children, Adam and Beth.

Contents

We have been interested in reincarnation for many years, and we have experienced many past-life regressions ourselves, so some of the regressions that you'll read about in this book are ours. Through meeting and working with a past-life regression therapist who later became a very good friend of ours, we recognized what our true life path should be, and thus we became healers and working psychic mediums. These days, Krys is also a past-life therapist and a hypnotherapist.

Before we personally explored the possibility of having lived before, and therefore of being able to live again, we both had a terrible fear of dying. We struggled with the thought that one of us would die and leave the other alone, and this worried us so much that we didn't like to be separated at all. Yes, we both went out to work, but we made sure the other was always safe. Our colleagues referred to us as being "joined at the hip," which is quite amusing because we are actually joined as souls! When we recognized that we've always been together throughout our past lives, we realized that life was indeed everlasting and that we would always be together, no matter what. Once we knew that, we were no longer afraid of dying or of one of us being left alone.

The other major issue we addressed in our lives was our career paths. We were both senior managers working for large organizations, with the associated stresses, strains, long working hours, and little leisure time. We were both disillusioned with our careers, and we were looking for ways to improve our health prospects as well as work in a much more meaningful and person-centered way. Krys had always been an intuitive healer, curing friends' and family members' headaches and healing our children when they hurt themselves, and we both had done some training in complementary therapies, including massage, reflexology, and Shiatsu—but none of these fully met our expectations.

During our past-life regressions, we discovered that we had been healers in many previous lives, and while we had already been drawn to healing in this life, we had not yet found the holistic solution we were looking for. However, we were inspired to keep looking. Our friend Moira Veevers, who is our regression therapist, finally persuaded us to visit her friend, who was a classical kinesiologist (that is, someone trained in the science of human movement, which is used for complementary health purposes). After that, we went on to train as classical kinesiologists ourselves, and we have never looked back. This isn't a book about kinesiology, although kinesiology plays a role in past-life therapy. In this book, we want to let you in on some of our past-life secrets and introduce you to the fascinating world of reincarnation, so that you can use it to access your own past lives and understand the legacy that past experiences have left buried in your psyche.

What Is Reincarnation?

1

The reincarnation belief system states that after death the soul or spirit is reborn into a new body. Most people believe that we can be reborn only into a human body, but some traditions include animal lives. For example, the Hindu tradition states that we can reincarnate from animals into humans and vice versa. A human being could have been, say, a seagull in a previous life.

The essence of reincarnation is that we progress as souls, so during each life we develop different areas of our personalities or characters. The belief is that through our different lives we experience all that life has to offer, whether wealth or poverty, health or disease, ignorance or a good education. We can be male or female, black or white, nobility or peasant. We can belong to any and every religious organization, and we can espouse every nonreligious belief, and every political view. We can live in every culture so that we experience, understand, and eventually accept all cultures, at which point a further human incarnation is not necessary and we can ascend to a pure spirit form.

This belief system is an ancient one. Several religions recognize it as central to their beliefs, and many pagans, and those who follow New Age beliefs or such esoteric philosophies as the Kabbala and Gnosticism, believe in reincarnation. There is also debate among Spiritualists—whose belief is that the spirit exists distinct from matter—some of whom hold this as a belief and some of whom do not.

Discovering Your Previous Incarnations

There are a number of ways to access information about your previous incarnations. These are the most commonly used methods.

Recession

Recession occurs when a therapist who is treating you in a complementary health or spiritual manner comes across past-life themes that are relevant to you in this lifetime. Whether the discovery is the result of a deliberate search for past-life problems or an accidental occurrence, the therapist will determine ways of addressing those themes.

Note that this is different from *regression*, described below. In *recession*, the therapist is intuitively accessing information from your past lives in order to heal you in the present.

Reading

Instead of looking at your present or future life, a psychic or medium can give you a reading in which he or she accesses information about your past lives and gives you information about one or more previous incarnations that are relevant to or resonate with patterns in your life now.

Regression

Regression is the process of going back into your past lives to retrieve past-life memories. This is different from recession because it is you, yourself, not the therapist, who recalls and discovers the past life.

To recall one or more of your own past lives in this way, you must be hypnotized by a qualified therapist. It is normally only under hypnosis that deliberate regression comes into play. It does so because hypnosis places individuals in a calm, receptive state, which allows memories of a past life to be brought to mind. While you are under hypnosis, you may also remember something about your life between lives or, as we call it, time spent in the discarnate realm.

Spontaneous Recall

Spontaneous recall happens when an event, situation, person, place, or emotion triggers your recall of a previous incarnation without any prior intent on your part to do so.

Dreams and Feelings

You may have dreams that relate to a past life, so it is worth taking particular note of any recurring dreams, because these may

be connected to past-life events. Our friend Vicki used to dream of a previous life in a South American jungle, where she sometimes had to cross a narrow ravine via a wood and rope bridge. In Vicki's dream, she was always nervous when crossing this fragile bridge; and rightly so, as it happened. One day, she was gingerly crossing the bridge while holding her small daughter by the hand, when one of the wooden slats broke. The little girl started to slip through the gap, but Vicki pulled her back up and then ran back to their village with the crying child in her arms. Vicki discovered later that her little daughter's arm had been broken in the fall.

One day in present life, Vicki's daughter told her that she a recurring dream that bothered her. In her dream, she was a little girl who lived with her family in a South American jungle, and that she had slipped through a wood and rope bridge, and only been saved from death by her mother hauling her back up. Interestingly, Vicki's daughter once broke her arm badly in this life, and it has never been quite right since.

• • •

Everyone's reincarnation story is different. We'll share our story in the next chapter, so you can get an idea of past lives and how information about them is obtained in regression sessions.

Jass's
Story

2

We all know what it is like to reach a crossroads in our lives and not know which way to go. The following story is one that showed me (Jass) the answer to a problem that was facing me. It showed me that money (or, in my case, a good salary) is not a guarantee of happiness, and that one can be happier with less income but better circumstances.

My first ever regression session was about ten years ago. Krys and I were both in stressful jobs, our children were young adults, and from time to time, Krys and I had reflected on the meaning of life and our frustration in our jobs. I had intended to be in the line of work I was in for a couple of years to get myself on my feet financially so that I could do something I enjoyed, but fifteen years later, having climbed the career ladder and being relatively well paid, I found it harder and harder to make the change. In spite of the good salaries we enjoyed, we were so exhausted at the end of each week that we didn't really feel the benefit from the money we earned—most of which seemed to go toward paying bills anyway. It was at this point that I had my first past-life regression, in which I vividly experienced two very different lives. The substance of them is related here.

Looking at my clothing on entering my past life, I discovered that I was wearing a dark green riding habit, smartly tailored to fit my young adult female figure. Going back to an even earlier stage of this past life, I found myself as a young girl hiding in a tree. From this viewpoint, I could see a very large house and surrounding estate. I knew that the estate belonged to my father and that I lived there with my mother and father and many servants. I looked into one of the windows of the big house, straight

into the schoolroom, where my governess was pacing up and down in anger. I
laughed to myself, knowing that she was
waiting for me. I was meant to be in the
classroom having a boring lesson with
her, but I was far happier outside, having
escaped for the day.

Moving forward in that lifetime, I
found myself in my early twenties. Once
again, I was wearing my favorite green
riding habit. Mother and I had long since
stopped arguing about this, but my
mother's continued displeasure was plain to see, as she would
have much preferred me to wear the gowns that adorned the fig-
ures of other young ladies in the southern states of America.

Around this time, my teenage cousin came to visit. The following days and weeks were the happiest of that life. My cousin
and I spent many happy hours riding horses all over my father's
estate. Over the next few months, I fell deeply in love with her.
My cousin and I would often go out to the farthest reaches of
the estate in order to have some privacy, but a family servant
spied on us and told my father that he had seen the two of us
in an unseemly embrace! My cousin was sent packing, and I was
devastated.

The next scene found me somewhat later in that lifetime,
working near the front lines in the American Civil War, nursing
injured men and being obsessed about germs. Moving forward a
few years, I found myself back at home. I was told that my cousin

had married a man, and in my absence, my father had arranged a marriage for me to a suitable man of good family. I flatly refused to marry; if I could not be with my one true love, I would not be with anyone. I remember standing at the top of the stairs arguing with my father. In the heat of the moment, he pushed me and I fell down the stairs. Following a long period of recovery, I was able to move around once again, but my broken right hip never healed properly, I never rode again, and thereafter I walked only with the aid of a stick.

Moving on once again in that lifetime, I found myself working as a governess to two children in a family who were friends of my father. This family was sympathetic to me, although the real reason for my wanting to leave home was never discussed. The schoolroom was fun, as the two children were great characters, and I gave them interesting challenges and tests to complete. I also taught them to climb up door frames in opposite corners of the room!

On the last day in that lifetime, I was an old woman sitting in a rocking chair, still living with the family that had taken me in as a governess. Even though the children were grown, they treated me like one of the family. It was not the same as having my own family, though. My final act, as I was dying, was to refuse to drink a horrible potion that the doctor offered me.

I quickly moved on from that lifetime to another past life, which found me as a young boy living in a small rural community where I spent most of my time outside. Home was a very small, cold hut, with mother by the hearth and brothers and sisters all around. Food was very scarce, and I really felt the cold. I had hunger pains in my stomach, and I felt the roughness of my clothes and the itching of the bugs in my hair and on my skin! As I moved through that lifetime, I experienced a life of poverty but lots of family love. I cleared stones from a field, and I killed a hare with a good shot from my sling and proudly presented it to mother for the pot. I was allowed the special bonus of keeping the skin, which I used to patch my shoes and make a new hat.

Brothers and sisters were plentiful, with new ones coming regularly until, eventually, father failed to return from his work at sea. Soon I was a teenager, and I began to be more useful by going fishing in a log boat with other boys my age. The feel of the slippery fish guts in the bottom of the boat and the stink of fish were disgusting. I must have looked for a way out of this kind of work, because when I moved forward in that life, I was working as an apprentice in a small shipbuilding shed on the coast.

I vividly recalled one morning when I ran happily to work as the sun rose over the horizon. I made sure I got to the shed first and got everything ready for the older men. I felt so happy to be doing that job and so glad to be finished with fish guts. I learned new woodworking skills, but one day I seriously cut my left leg. An older man took me to the village healer, a wise old woman who put a paste over the cut and gave me more paste for the next few days. I healed remarkably well and continued to learn the ways of working wood for making ships. I felt a deep attachment to the village healer and often visited her on my way home, taking her a little gift each time I went, much to my mother's annoyance. Food was scarce and family should have come first, but I reminded my mother that without the healer I would have lost my leg and may have died.

On the last day of that lifetime, I was still a young man, on my own in the shipbuilding shed, moving logs around. A log high in the pile broke free and fell on me, crushing my chest. I watched as I moved out of my body and saw that I had drawn my last ragged breath before anyone arrived to help me.

After those two past-life experiences, I was asked to look back over them and reflect on what they meant to me now. The contrast between the two lives—one rich but emotionally poor, the other impoverished but filled with love and happiness—gave me a clear understanding, in a way that I had never felt before, that money does not guarantee happiness.

I was asked whether I recognized anyone in these two past lifetimes. I saw that my partner in this lifetime was my cousin and lover in the first lifetime and also the village healer in the second. So, be aware that your soul mate in this lifetime is not always your mate in other lifetimes. The two children I taught in the first lifetime are the two children Krys and I have in this lifetime, and they came into my life when I was at a similar age in both lives. After I had experienced this regression, Krys told me that before we met, and when our current children were very young, they also had climbed up the door frames and sat at the top of the doorways talking to each other. Krys had never done this, and she had never understood where they had gotten the idea, but I had done this often as a child myself, though I had never known anyone else to do it.

The reference to the American Civil War gives a date for the first of these two past lives. After the regression, I looked it up and found out that the war had lasted from 1861 to 1865. Pictures of the uniforms were exactly as I had seen them in my regression, which shows that what I had experienced was authentic.

Now, many years later, I have left my old career. Krys and I are self-employed as therapists and psychic mediums. This is so much more personally fulfilling than our previous careers were, and although we no longer have the security of a monthly salary, we are happier now than ever before!

Many Lives, Many Experiences

3

When you first embark on discovering your previous incarnations, it is tempting to hope for a lifetime in which you were a great and famous person. In our experience, this rarely happens. There have been very many more ordinary people than famous ones, and the ratio of ordinary to famous is enormous. Based on the laws of probability, it is highly unlikely that you were one of the few famous ones. However, looking at your past lives is not about being famous or whether a previous incarnation has been written about in history books. What is important to recognize is that each incarnation that a soul experiences is a chapter in the book of that soul's journey. In one incarnation you may be rich; in another you may be reasonably comfortable or even extremely poor. From each life, you learn something that your soul takes with it beyond the end of that physical life and into the next life.

Before you start your journey of self-discovery through your previous incarnations, you may wonder whether you have been rich or poor in past lives. Have you also wondered about being a different gender in past lives than you are in this lifetime? Living as male in some lives and female in others and having a wide variety of roles and experiences gives your soul a great opportunity to appreciate life from many different aspects. Therefore, whether you are male or female this time around, you have probably been both several times before. Able-bodied or disabled? You have probably experienced much of both before as well. Whether you are European, Australian, Asian, North or South American, Middle Eastern, or African, you have experienced life in other cultures before. You may well find that you have lived many different lives, thus giving your soul the opportunity to experience a diverse range of capabilities and control over your own life—or the lack of it.

It is also likely that you have experienced a variety of roles and responsibilities in your various lifetimes. Imagine lifetimes as a milkmaid, a laborer, a powerful property owner, a cook, an artist, a scientist, a law enforcer, a farmer, a nun, a priest, or a sailor. These

are just a few of the roles that you may have experienced. In some lifetimes, you may have been playing a supporting role for another soul. In this kind of incarnation, you may not have experienced much opportunity for personal growth. It is a little like thinking of a life as a play. Occasionally you take a supporting role rather than the lead. In most of your lifetimes, you will be the lead, and there will be supporting actors to help you with your life challenges, but none of us exists in a vacuum, so you will also have played a supporting role in other lifetimes in order to help others along their path. That will certainly also be the case in this lifetime.

Each lifetime gives you a unique opportunity to live that life to the full, to develop your positive characteristics and qualities and to overcome your challenges. What matters is not the person you have been or the amount of power or wealth you have had, but what you did, how you did it, how you related to other people, and how you made the most of your opportunities for your own soul to grow and develop.

Before you embark on your personal journey of discovery, be open to the different types of lives that you might have had. Being open to the possibilities will prevent you from putting a limit on the incarnations you can access. If you believe, for example, that you *only* could have been wealthy and influential, that belief will limit you from experiencing the true range of your past lives. Experiencing your full personal variety of incarnations has the effect of helping you to understand that we really are all one big community and that in any lifetime you could have been in anyone else's position. Really feeling this can be a massive revelation to you if you have not thought this way before.

Why Look At Previous Lives?

There are many reasons why you may be drawn to look into your previous incarnations. You could be experiencing ongoing health challenges, fears or phobias, relationship or intimacy problems, or financial or property issues that are connected to a previous incarnation. These may have been carried through to this current

life for you to finally reconcile.
Alternatively, you may be fascinated
by a particular period in time or a
particular part of the world or a culture that you have not experienced
in this lifetime; that means that it is
likely that you lived during that time
or in that culture in the past. Some
people are merely curious about
who they might have been during
previous incarnations, the lives they
lived and the family and friends who were around them.

Have I Been Here Before?

The fact that you have chosen to read this book means that, for
you, the answer to this question is "yes." It's because you have lived
before that you have been drawn to read a book such as this, so
you can be sure that something you read here will resonate with
you. Our view is that there are very, very small numbers of new
souls generated from what we call the Source, which others may
refer to as God, the Divine, the Great Spirit, or the Creator. For this
reason, the majority of us have lived at least one previous life.

Will I Be Here Again?

The answer to this question varies. It may be that you are reaching the end of your human incarnations; you may have learned

everything you need to from this unique and beautiful planet of ours, and you may be ready to ascend to the higher spirit realms. Alternatively, one of two things may happen: You may still be on your soul journey and therefore will come back and learn more after a stay in the discarnate world at the end of this lifetime, or you may remain in the discarnate world and enter the higher spirit realms, where you will have a greater understanding of the meaning, reality, and diversity of human life. So enjoy the wonderful opportunities there are for us as humans to live, laugh, and love and, especially, to learn and grow.

Will I Be the Same as I Am Now?

You may or may not be the same as you are now. You will still be you, but you may come back in a different gender, and you may or may not repeat some of the things that you've done in your current life. Indeed, there may be some themes that carry on from life to life.

Looking back over previous lives will show whether that will prove to be the case with you or not. Your friends and relatives may still be with you, but in a different pattern; for example, a friend may become a sister, or a brother may become a father, uncle, or son. You may do some things differently, possibly because the circumstances of your future life will be different from the current one or because you may have learned something useful from the previous life and avoid making the same mistakes again.

Recession

4

R ecession literally means the act of going backward. Past-life recession is a very effective technique that is used by quali-fied therapists to identify aspects from one or more of your previ-ous incarnations that are relevant to a present-day issue that you might want to address. These past-life aspects of the issue are taken into account in the therapeutic work that occurs during the session.

Kinesiology

Kinesiology is an excellent therapy to use for accessing relevant information from previous incarnations. Kinesiology works by using muscle testing, usually using a muscle in an individual's arm, as a means of biofeedback. This is not about the strength of the muscle; instead, it captures a moment in time when something significant interrupts the nerve messaging between the muscle and the brain. Muscle testing in effect taps into the whole knowl-edge database of the individual, not just what is contained in his or her conscious mind. Using this muscle-testing biofeedback tech-nique, a kinesiologist can determine the most important issue for the individual at that moment in time, and then he or she can go on to identify all relevant aspects of the issue. Once the informa-tion has been gathered, the best remedies for the individual can be determined.

In the simplest of scenarios, muscle testing can be used to identify foods to which the individual has become intolerant. To do this, the kinesiologist would ask the individual to hold his or her arm in a position to partially engage a particular muscle. The kinesiologist would then apply light downward pressure to the arm, which in normal circumstances would be easy for the individual to counter, allowing the individual to keep his or her arm in the same position. However, if the person is intolerant to the food, the muscle will easily give way. This is not about the muscle becoming weak but about capturing the moment when the nerve message to that muscle is interrupted for a few moments.

This reaction can also be caused by stress, an emotional challenge, or a physical or biochemical problem. This muscle testing technique is useful to many kinds of therapists; for instance, an herbalist might use it to find an individual's best herbal combination and exact dosage.

All kinesiologists use muscle testing, but kinesiology itself offers much more than just muscle testing. Fully qualified kinesiologists are trained in a wide range of additional techniques that are used in conjunction with muscle testing.

For most people, seeing a kinesiologist involves the practitioner and individual agreeing on the challenges that are to be worked on during the session. Muscle testing may also clearly show the kinesiologist what challenges the subconscious mind feels are the priorities. The therapist also includes relevant events

and emotions found through muscle testing, and then uses the muscle test to find the best remedies.

Remedies can be many and varied, and they may include balancing the chakras, tapping the meridians, or giving emotional support in the form of flower remedies. Some therapists use positive affirmations along with acupressure points, herbal remedies, vitamins, minerals, and other complementary remedies.

As well as being used to capture information about current issues, kinesiology can be used to gather information about situations that occurred in the individual's current lifetime as well as those that arise from previous lives. By using a technique called "age recession," the therapist uses muscle testing to identify significant ages within the individual's current lifetime when things happened that have resulted in mental or physical discomfort.

Trained kinesiologists can use an extension of the age-recession technique that allows the therapist to go farther back into a previous life in order to pick up information from before the individual's current physical lifetime. This process allows the kinesiologist to access and include past-life information in the therapeutic work. This does not involve an altered state of consciousness for the individual, as would occur during hypnotism. However, it often happens that the individual feels the emotion of the past life that is being explored. The individual may release the emotions by crying or laughing, and he or she often recognizes the connection of the past life to his or her experiences in this lifetime.

Some very sensitive individuals also get some sense of what actually happened in that past life, but most individuals don't, despite the fact that they are suffering the effects of a past-life event. This is frustrating for some people, as they become excited by the idea and want details about the past life right there and then. Muscle testing can reveal whether it would be right for the individual to look into the past life in detail. What can and should be done at any one time depends on a number of circumstances, and only the therapist can determine the best way forward.

The knowledge gathered using muscle testing may include information about when and where a previous lifetime occurred. Our bodies know much more about us than we give them credit for, and a qualified kinesiologist can use bodily reactions as a very sensitive, accurate, and holistic way of tapping into an individual. Because it taps into the whole knowledge database, kinesiology is a powerful tool for helping individuals resolve any kind of issue. Complex issues often have multiple aspects, and this kind of therapeutic work can be a bit like peeling an onion! Many conditions have a physical, biochemical, and emotional or spiritual aspect. We see this a lot in problems such as stress, irritable bowel syndrome, and chronic fatigue. Sometimes only certain aspects (those the individual can reasonably cope with at the time) turn up during a session, so it may be necessary for an individual to have more than one session and for the individual and the therapist to take the process at the right pace for that individual.

Other Methods

It is entirely possible for past-life issues to be discovered in other types of therapy sessions. We have known this to happen in reflexology, which stimulates reflex points on the hands and feet to promote self-healing, and in bodywork therapies, such as massage, which can trigger cellular memory release. However the realization of the involvement of previous incarnations comes about, it is up to the individual and therapist to agree how best to further explore these issues. Sometimes it may be right to address these issues within the current therapy session, but in other circumstances, it is much better to explore the past-life aspects in a separate therapy session that is specifically tailored to address such issues.

Remember:

When challenges from an individual's previous incarnations are picked up in therapeutic work, their relevance will strike a chord with that individual. Recession is a fantastic way of accessing past-life issues that have a bearing on physical or emotional pain.

A Recession Session: Brenda

To demonstrate the way a kinesiology session can include past-life issues, let us use the example of an individual whom we will call Brenda. Brenda felt that people who are close to her always leave her. When someone suffers from feelings of abandonment, relevant information can come from this lifetime, but it can also come from issues that emerge from previous incarnations. In Brenda's kinesiology session, muscle testing identified that the issue of feeling abandoned was the priority issue to be worked on.

Muscle testing showed that in her current relationship, Brenda got upset on one particular occasion when a family crisis arose and her partner chose to go to work rather than stay home and help her deal with it. For some people, this would not have been a big deal, but for Brenda, it drilled into complex feelings that stemmed from the past and gave rise to feelings of abandonment, resentment, and anger.

The next challenge for Brenda was that her youngest child had recently left home, so her nest was empty. Her children were all making their own way in the world, and like many adult children, phone calls became few and far between. Although she was happy to see that they were all getting on well, their inconsistency about staying in touch gave rise to feelings of resentment, and this made Brenda feel left behind and unappreciated, after having put a lot of time and energy into raising her children.

Earlier in this lifetime, Brenda had gone through experiences that also contributed to her feeling of abandonment. These experiences were discovered using the age-recession technique, which allows the therapist to identify relevant ages and their associated problems. Muscle testing identified that when Brenda was seven years old, her father wasn't there for her in the way that Brenda needed him to be. Her associated feelings of abandonment and helplessness were picked up from this age. On talking with Brenda, the therapist learned that her parents split up when she was seven, that her father left the family home, and that she had missed him a lot.

During the age-recession session, the therapist found that the age of twelve also appeared to be relevant. At this age, there seemed to be feelings of abandonment, grief, and sadness. Brenda confirmed that this was exactly how she felt at the age of twelve, when her beloved grandmother died. Brenda had been accustomed to going to her grandmother's house every day after school until her mother picked her up after work. This was a very special time for Brenda, as her grandmother would listen to her stories about school and spoil her with tea and cake. The experiences from this lifetime were in themselves a heavy load for Brenda to bear, but when the therapist added these experiences to those of her previous incarnations, the residual feelings, issues, and challenges that she has brought from these past lives into her present one became clear.

For instance, by using the extension of the age-recession technique, the therapist found that in one previous incarnation Brenda had lived in a primitive fishing community that had been struck by a terrible storm and that she was one of the few who survived this disaster. The feeling of abandonment from this trag-edy was identified and included in the session. The therapist dug into Brenda's past life to discover more detail about that lifetime, and it transpired that her father was the village elder of this fish-ing community.

Another past life showed itself as relevant. In it, all Brenda's children and her husband died, leaving her alone and unable to support herself. In times past and in less well-developed cultures, many people did not survive to adulthood, so it was common for a woman to have many children and for many of these children to die before they reached adulthood. This experience stays with some people and features in the way that they respond to current-day experiences. It turned out that one of Brenda's children in that life was her husband in this lifetime. She also discovered that her past life in the fishing village had been in an area of Africa that she had long felt drawn to and that she wanted to visit.

Finally, for Brenda, there was a third relevant past life. In this incarnation, she was a man who owned a very successful business with a brother. They traveled everywhere as traders, and they carried most of their goods and personal possessions with them. Their life was good and happy, but then the brother became greedy. One night when they were sleeping on a remote mountainside, the brother took both their horses and all their goods, and the male Brenda awoke the next day to find that he had been abandoned and left penniless, with no means of getting home.

With this myriad of abandonment issues, it is no wonder that Brenda was sensitive to any situation that invoked similar feelings for her. Having included all the relevant aspects for this issue of abandonment, the therapist used muscle testing to select remedies that would help Brenda resolve the issues associated with her feelings of abandonment. Brenda's experiences show how one or more previous incarnations can predispose a person to having some very sore spots in his or her psyche.

Readings

5

To get a sense of what your past lives were like, you need someone who can "read" your previous incarnations. In a past-life reading, a reader gives you information about one or more previous incarnations. Depending on how the reader works, this information may come from a spiritual guide, or the reader might pick up on your past life from your aura or energy field.

When a reader gives you a past-life reading, it is likely to start with people, places, and events that relate to your current lifetime, probably starting with a significant event. Then the reader will start to move back to a previous life, possibly starting the reading during your childhood in the previous life, and then moving forward and picking up as much relevant information as possible. You should not expect to feel any emotion relating to the incarnation. It may be that the incarnation in question doesn't have any special significance to you, but if the story does resonate strongly for you, and if it brings up similar events or feelings that are issues in your life now, it may bring up emotions and feelings for you.

If you do not feel a connection with what the reader tells you about your previous incarnation, then you might want to double-check that the reader is truly connecting with you. To do this, you can ask the reader to give you information about yourself that you can validate, such as news about what is happening in your life right now or about something from your past in the current lifetime. In short, this must be information that you can recognize. Most readers do not like to switch between current and past-life information too quickly, as it can confuse them and make it hard for them to pick up relevant information.

In practice, when you have a past-life reading, we recommend that you ensure that the reader has a good connection to you right at the start of the reading, before any past-life information is accessed. Most often, this will be the case, but occasionally even the best of readers can misfire, because no reader can connect with every person who comes in for a reading. Sometimes the reader is not right for the individual, so he or she recommends that the individual consult someone else. Sometimes a reader can't make a good connection on that day but is able to do so on another.

Usually the reader will make a great connection with your energy, giving you information you can understand and validate from your current lifetime. After this, the reader will move backward with confidence to a previous incarnation. A good connection to your present situation will also help connect to a relevant past life, because the past-life circumstances will be relevant to your current situation.

An Imaginary Reading

In this imaginary reading, the reader is female and the individual is male.

Let us assume that Krys is doing the reading. At the start of the reading, the reader connects with the individual and says something that only the individual can confirm, for example, "I see that you have recently clipped the nails of your two dogs." The individual confirms that he did this the previous day. The reader then goes on to state that the individual is in the process of applying for a new job, and the individual verifies this information also. The reader is now confident that she has established a good connection with the individual and moves on to access information from a previous incarnation.

The reading goes something like this:

"I see you in the desert, and there is a vast expanse of sand all around you. You are on the side of a very big sand dune, and you are trying to get to the top.

"Going back to earlier in that lifetime, I see you as a young boy living with your family as members of a nomadic desert tribe. Your tribe travels a set route each year. You stop at places to find food and water. Some of these places are also places where members of your tribe can meet people and trade with them. You have a mother and father and two older sisters. I see that you love to be with the animals. From an early age, you take care of the camels for the tribe along with another boy who is of a similar age to you.

"I see you now as a young man. You are working with the hunting birds that the tribe uses to help them gather food. You look after the birds and you help train them. I feel that this is something you really enjoy doing and that your birds are excellent hunters. As time moves on in this life, I feel you become restless and bored with traveling the same old route year after year.

"I now once again see the scene I first saw of you in the desert, on the side of a large sand dune trying to get to the top. You have your favorite bird with you. I see that there is a camp of tents in a shallow valley behind you; this is where your tribe has stopped for the night. As the sun starts to set in the evening sky, you reach the top of the dune. Standing there, you look across the vast landscape. Talking quietly to your bird, you ask it to show you the direction you should take. The bird flies off to the west, beyond the route your tribe travels. When the bird returns to you, the next question you put to it is, How far away is this place? The bird flies up in the air and flies around your head in two complete circles. A circle to your tribe denotes the moon and the passing of twenty-eight days. You decide that it is time for you to strike out on your own.

"As the story of this past life unfolds, I see that you bid good-bye to your family and friends and set off west with your own belongings, your camel, and your two birds of prey. You travel west for two full cycles of the moon, on the final day reaching a large town farther west than your tribe normally goes. Here you settle down and use your skill in working with hunting birds to

make a good life for yourself. You meet and fall deeply in love with a local girl. You marry the love of your life and have three good, strong children."

• • •

After the reading, the individual may feel a strong relationship between this story and the point that he has reached in his current life, and reflection on this helps him see that instead of looking for a job with another company, what he really wants is to strike out on his own, and do something new. Thinking about what really makes him happy, the individual realizes that what he really wants is to work with animals and he sees that he has thought about this before but had dismissed the idea. Now that the knowledge is firmly lodged in his mind, he is filled with enthusiasm, and he decides to start looking for exactly the right job, even if it means moving to another location.

This example demonstrates how information from a relevant past life can be of great interest and relevance to us in our current lives.

Proof of
Past Lives

6

How can we know that what we experience during a regression is truly a recall of a previous life? Well, the best way is to obtain evidence that you can verify after the session. There has been much written about children who remember a very recent past life, giving details of their past-life home and family. Their current families then locate the place and the previous family and confirm that their knowledge is absolutely correct. In this chapter, we include three of our own experiences that give good evidence.

The Coaching Inn

In a past-life regression I (Jass) clearly recalled a lifetime in which I was a coach driver. I drove the coach on a major coaching route somewhere around Shrewsbury in Shropshire, in the west of England. My sweetheart lived in a coaching inn run by her family, and I clearly recalled a scene outside the coaching inn. When we were courting, my sweetheart worked as a maid in "the big

house" which was down the road, around the bend, and up a long driveway from the coaching inn. On days when I passed this way, I would stop in at the coaching inn. Then, if it was at a time when my sweetheart was working, I would stop the coach at the gates of the big house, she would run down the driveway with an apple for me, and I would give her a flower and, of course, a kiss! This was a very simple but special life to me. My sweetheart was, of course, Krys, as you may have guessed. Eventually we both took over the running of the coaching inn, and her aged parents and the two of us lived in very cramped but happy conditions in the small coaching house.

About three years after this past-life regression, Krys and I were driving through the countryside near Shrewsbury, taking a long, leisurely diversion on a trip to the north of England. We had a rare free day to ourselves, so we were enjoying a drive through countryside that we had never been through before—as far as we were aware! Imagine our surprise when a road suddenly became very familiar to me, and just as I said this to Krys, the old inn that was exactly as I had seen it in my past-life regression session came into view. We stopped the car a little farther along the road and I told Krys that, if this was indeed the place, on the right-hand side of the road, just around the bend, we would see a long driveway to the big house. We drove slowly along the road, and just after the bend, set back on the right, there was a massive old house with a long driveway leading up to it. It had been converted into offices, but the feeling of familiarity was still overwhelming.

a past-life regression, I (Jass) experienced a lifetime in
erset, in southwest England. Krys and I had both been young
girls in a little village. As we grew to adulthood, we fell in love.
Our attempts to keep our relationship secret failed, and, fearing
for our lives, Krys's father took us one night in his cart to live with
a female cousin of his. This woman and her husband and son took
us both in, and we lived on their cider farm for the rest of that
lifetime. I clearly recalled life on the farm, the farm buildings, a
local mill, and the walk to the nearby town of Glastonbury. At the
time of this regression, I had never been to Somerset.

About six years after I experienced this past-life regression,
Krys and I met a lovely woman at a workshop that we were
attending. We all quickly felt a deep attachment and became good
friends. When we visited her, we found that she lived in a little

village just outside Glastonbury. After getting to know our friend better and sharing our thoughts on issues such as reincarnation, I told her about the past life that I had experienced somewhere around Glastonbury. She found this fascinating, and without saying much more about my story, she suggested we go for a little drive around the local countryside.

She told us to turn down a narrow country lane and suggested that we both look at the view out of the right side of the car. Just a little farther along the road we saw the entrance to an old farm, and it was exactly as I had seen it in my regression. I knew what was in each building and where the orchard was in relation to the house. The entrance arch was quite distinctive and very old, and the arrangement of buildings around the central courtyard was just as I had recalled it. We then drove back to our new friend's house; she told us that the house she lived in was built on land that used to be a part of the apple orchard. Moreover, the apple orchard belonged to the cider farm that we had just seen. How amazing is that?

Prehistoric Ways

During one past-life regression, I (Jass) experienced an incarnation in southern Europe in an area that is now in Portugal, just inland from the Atlantic coast. At the time of this regression, I had never visited Portugal, but I had wanted to since I was a teenager. The past life was in prehistoric times, and it was very basic, with food being the overriding issue. I lived in a cave with two adult men, an adult female, a boy, and an older girl. I was a girl of

about ten years old. The woman, boy, girl, and I felt like family, but our relationships to the adult men in the group were not clear. They slept by the fire near the entrance to the cave; the rest of us slept nearer the back. We all had animal skins as clothing and bed covers.

One scene stayed with me so clearly that after the regression session I felt compelled to draw what I had been doing. I was cleaning a large animal skin. The way I cleaned it was by stretching it within an upright wooden frame. I had made holes around the edges of the skin and had used animal gut as thread to pull the skin tight within the large wooden frame. It seemed that the skin had been left to dry for some time and I was now using a sharp-edged flat stone to scrape it clean. It seems disgusting now, but I clearly recalled getting some fat from the skin caught under my fingernail and eating it. I clearly considered this a bonus for doing this shoulder-aching job! I suppose we were so hungry that even a scrap of raw fat was welcome sustenance. The frame was taller than I was, and I had to balance on strategically placed rocks to reach the top of the skin.

The way I cleaned this skin was very clear to me, but it was very different from the way I might have imagined skins to be cleaned. If anyone had asked me I would have said that to do this job, skins were laid out on hard ground and worked on by an individual crouching over them. Years after this past-life regression, while watching television, I saw an archaeology program that was looking at prehistory. This program showed how ancient people cleaned skins, and—you guessed it—the picture was exactly as I had drawn it! I was so surprised that I ran to find my drawing, and I showed it to everyone else in the room. This felt like real evidence to me, as my vision had seemed so odd at the time, but I'd actually drawn the cleaning method in the exact way that it had been done so long ago.

Fears and Phobias

7

Some fears and phobias can have their roots in a past life. There are two types of fears and phobias that relate to past-life experience: those that are present at birth and those that start suddenly at a particular age. For example, one person may always have been scared of water, while another person may have started to be fearful of water only when she reached her teens. Both types of fear can have their roots in a past life.

Fears and phobias that come about suddenly may relate to a traumatic experience that occurred in a past life at the same age as the onset of the present-life phobia. For example, someone may have witnessed a house fire in which he or she lost loved ones when the person was twenty-five years old in a previous life. In this case, the person may start to fear fire from the age of twenty-five in the present lifetime. When a fear or phobia is present from birth, it may be the result of a number of lifetimes in which the same problem has occurred. Only now may the individual be able to overcome a problem such as this that is rooted in the past.

Fear of Snakes

Cathy had been afraid of snakes since about the age of ten—so much so that she absolutely refused to go on vacation to any location where snakes might exist. She remembered looking at books on animals as a very young child and not being bothered by snakes, though she was curious about how they moved around without any legs. From around the time Cathy turned ten, though, the phobia started, and it soon started to cause Cathy real anxiety.

Once, against her better judgment, Cathy went on a walking holiday in South Wales, even though she had read that an animal liberation group had released snakes from a research facility into that area. All went well, as Cathy kept to the center of the path and stamped her feet loudly as she walked. Later she discovered that she had walked right past a snake. A friend had seen it but had kept quiet about it, as she knew how scared Cathy was. Even seeing snakes on television or reading a book that mentioned them would paralyze Cathy with fear.

Many people live with fears and phobias, and you may think that a phobia about snakes for a person in England, where snakes are quite rare, is best just left alone. Well, that was exactly how Cathy used to feel; she had even refused to have the kind of familiarization therapy in which an individual is forced to come face-to-face with his or her fears. She was amazed, therefore, when a past-life regression brought the issue up and helped her understand the root cause of this fear.

During the past-life regression, Cathy experienced a life in the Australian out-back, where she lived on a sheep farm. As a little girl, Cathy was too young to be of much use on the farm, so she became responsible for training the sheepdogs. Cathy absolutely loved this task, and she had a small number of very well-trained dogs. One dog in particular was her favorite, and they went everywhere together.

Life on the farm was hard and very basic. There was no inside plumbing, and the "bathroom" consisted of a dugout in a little hut at the end of a short path from the house. One day when Cathy was about ten years old, she was walking down this path with her dog at her side. Suddenly a snake that she must have disturbed took up an aggressive strike mode. Cathy's dog immediately went in to attack it, and the snake bit the dog and then slid off back into the scrubland beside the path. There was no one else around, as the farm was spread out over a lot of land. Cathy's mother, father, and older brothers were all away working on the land, but somehow she managed to pick the dog up and haul him up onto her shoulders. Cathy ran in a panic all the way to a neighbor who was good with animals. All her efforts were in vain, though; when she got to the neighbor, the precious dog was past saving, and he died. Cathy ran back to her family's farm, crying all the way, with her poor dead dog on her shoulders. This episode was significant because the thing that had really mattered in that lifetime was the way Cathy's beloved dog had died.

Experiencing this past life helped Cathy to understand where her fear had come from. It is significant that her fear of snakes in this lifetime started at the same age she was when her dog died from the snakebite in her past life. She now accepts that her fear had a logical basis in that life but is now redundant. Cathy says that even now she would not choose to be near a snake but that she can read a book that mentions them and she no longer freezes with fear if she sees them on television. Cathy even takes walks in areas where there is a remote possibility of coming across an adder or a grass snake. She now has a more balanced approach, and while she feels that snakes have a right to live, she is more than happy to keep her distance!

Fear of Death

Many people fear death. Some fear the manner in which they may pass over—in other words, the dying process itself—while others fear being separated from loved ones, and yet others fear what the discarnate realm holds for them.

Fear of the dying process itself is a very logical one, although as working mediums, and having communicated with many souls in spirit, we know that those who have passed over tend not to dwell on the actual dying process itself. That may be because it was such a tiny part of their lives and they feel that the manner of their passing is no longer important. However, they often let us know the circumstances of their death, frequently showing where

they passed and whether they were ill beforehand. Having experienced regression ourselves, we have recalled the dying process, so we know what it feels like.

In times gone by, when there was more fighting, more starvation, less medicine, and fewer people living comfortable lives, we probably all passed to spirit in difficult ways. Some passed in tragic ways and others in relatively comfortable ways, but in these days of modern medicine, pain relief is much better, so our passing is likely to be painless (provided there is no violence involved, such as a fatal car accident), although it may be emotionally painful for our loved ones to witness.

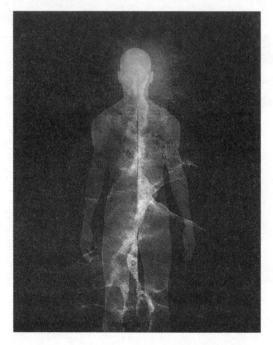

The fear of the discarnate realm is one area where past-life regression can help. Regression can take you to the discarnate realm and allow you to talk with your guides and helpers more clearly, so that you can allay your fears. The discarnate realm is a place of love and joy rather than retribution and sadness. You may have done things in this life that you are not particularly proud of, and it is far better to make retribution and make positive changes in this lifetime so that you no longer do things that make you or others unhappy. This is far better than worrying about what you will learn when you pass over to spirit. It is easier to take small steps to change and then to keep up the good work than it is to give yourself a moral makeover in one shot and then slide back to your more challenging ways. With counseling and support, people can make huge changes for the better in their lives.

Hypnotic Regression

8

For those of you who fear being separated from your loved ones, past-life regression can make a huge difference in your life. You will discover that your soul is eternal, that your loved ones will be with you again in spirit when you pass from this world, and that they will be with you again in future lives.

Although we describe certain methods of regression here, we recommend that you consult a qualified regression therapist for this kind of treatment. The following will show you what to do, which can be useful if you or a friend is already a qualified hypnotic therapist, or if you or a friend is training to become one.

Caution: If you have any history of mental health challenges, it is important that you seek professional advice before trying to put yourself into any kind of altered state.

While reading the following, the therapist should vary the tone and inflection of his or her voice. The following shows you how you can vary the emphasis on the words (in italics):

"Who are you?"
Your response

"Who *are* you?"
Your response

"*Who* are you?"
Your response

"Who are *you*?"
Your response

"Who are you?"

Your response

Your therapist will continue with these questions in a gentle and empathetic voice for around ten minutes. Don't be surprised; just listen and respond. When you look at the responses that your therapist notes down, you may find some surprising answers. If you gave a name, it may not be your own name from a past life; you could well be calling out to someone else.

You may wonder why we call this process hypnotic regression, when you don't feel the slightest bit hypnotized. This is because hypnotism is simply taking your mind into a slightly altered state so that your subconscious mind can be activated, rather than having your conscious mind blocking and controlling your thoughts. Your therapist's voice should be gentle and empathetic, allowing your subconscious mind to be accessed and encouraging the information to flow from you. Your first few responses will be stilted, but after a while you will reach your previous existences.

Guided Visualization

Another method that your therapist might try is a guided visualization that will relax you and encourage a receptive state of mind.

Tip: The series of three dots in a row (. . .) indicate places where the therapist should pause in the visualization.

- "Make sure you are sitting or lying comfortably, and close your eyes . . .

- "Take a deep breath in and out. . . and relax . . .

- "Now, just listen to the sound of my voice . . . and any noise you hear simply takes you deeper into peace and deeper into relaxation . . .

- "Now, just concentrate on your toes and your breathing . . . gentle, steady, rhythmic breaths . . . feeling warm, comfortable, and relaxed . . . and as you take those gentle breaths in and out. . . with each breath feel your toes start to relax . . .

- "Concentrate on your toes now . . . and with each breath in . . . just imagine you are bringing that relaxing feeling in your toes further into your feet. . . into your ankles and your heels . . .

- "Feel the whole of your feet now relaxed . . . and as you take more relaxing breaths, this feeling of relaxation travels into your shins and calves . . . traveling up your legs . . . to your thighs and into your hips . . .

- "Feel the whole of your legs now relaxed . . .

- "Now, bring this warm, relaxing feeling into your lower back and stomach . . . and then into your upper back and chest . . . Even feel your shoulders relax now . . .

- "Just feel the whole of your body sinking into the bed [chair] you are lying [sitting] on . . . Feel warm, comfortable, and relaxed . . .

- "Now, allow that wonderful relaxing feeling to travel into your upper arms . . . and then into your elbows . . . to your lower arms and wrists, and into your hands and each of your fingers now . . .

- "Feeling warm, comfortable, and relaxed . . .

- "Bring that relaxing feeling back up your arms . . . into your shoulders once more . . . and then into your neck . . . Let your neck relax now; feel it supported and comfortable . . .

- "In addition, as your whole body feels relaxed, allow that relaxed feeling to finally travel into your jaw, your eyes and ears, and the whole of your head . . . Let your forehead relax.

- "I want you to enjoy this relaxing feeling . . . Simply feel yourself drifting with it as you start to imagine . . .

- "In your imagination, I want you to picture yourself on a beach. You're sitting in the sand. You can feel the sun on your face, a gentle breeze on your skin. There's not a cloud in the sky, and you are beautifully safe and relaxed . . .

- "Sit and listen to the sound of the waves as they come in and go out again . . .

- "Notice that your breathing is in sync with the waves . . . . As the waves roll in, you breathe in, and as the waves recede again, you breathe out. . . . That's in . . . and out. . . in . . . and out. . .

- "In addition, as you're sitting on this beach feeling the sand supporting you, you can hear the sound of the waves and you can hear the distant cry of the seabirds.

- "The sea is a lovely brilliant blue, and the sand is beautiful golden sand.

- "Just sit here for a moment and listen to the waves . . .

- "You know now that in a moment you're going to get up from where you're sitting, and you're going to make your way to a lower and magical part of this beach, a place where you can find your previous memories, memories that you had forgotten until now, but you are going to find them easy to remember, happy memories of happy times you have spent in the past.

- "Now, I want you to stand up from where you are sitting on the beach and feel the sand beneath your toes . . .

- "You start to walk along the water's edge, still feeling that gentle breeze on your face . . . and up ahead of you, you become aware of a wall . . . and in this wall is a gate . . .

- "You walk up to the gate and put your hands on it. . . You can feel the wood of the gate underneath your fingertips now, and you know that this is an ancient gate that has stood on this point for centuries . . .

- "You push the gate open, and it opens easily for you, and you become aware of a series of stone steps leading down to a lower part of the beach below . . . You know you are perfectly safe here, and you are feeling happy and relaxed as you step onto the first step . . . That's one . . .

- "You feel the stone beneath your feet, which is warmed by the heat of the sun, and you step on to the second step now . . . two . . . and down again to the third step . . . three . . . and down deeper to the fourth step . . . four. . . going deeper and deeper now to the fifth step . . . five . . . and deeper still to the sixth step . . . six . . .

- "And now deeper still as you step down again . . . seven . . . going deeper and deeper and feeling more and more calm and relaxed as you step down again . . . eight. . . and down another step . . . nine . . . and down to the last step now . . . ten . . .

- "You are feeling beautifully calm and relaxed . . . calm and relaxed . . . Now, as you find yourself on this lower part of the beach . . . you know that you are in a magical place here . . .

- "You can still feel the sand underneath your feet as you find yourself walking into a tunnel underneath the rocks now . . .

- "This tunnel is perfectly safe, and you know that you have been here before as you begin to walk along it . . .

- "This is the 'tunnel of time,' and you know that in here you will be able to access wonderful memories of lives . . . wonderful memories of lives you have lived before . . . You will be able to visit those lives for a brief time and bring those memories back into your mind . . .

- "You will remember a happy and wonderful life filled with love . . . a happy and wonderful life filled with love . . . as you walk along the time tunnel. . .

- "This tunnel is well lit and is warm and soothing . . .

- Take a look around you now as you walk along this time tunnel, and you will start to pass some doors now . . . doors cut into the sides of the tunnel . . .

- "You know that you are going to find that special door. . . Feel drawn to that door now as you drift along this time tunnel. . . and you will see now that one door seems special to you somehow . . . one door feels special . . .

- "Take a look at the door or feel the door now . . .

- What color does it seem to be? . . . From what material is the door made? . . .

- "Find yourself now at that special door, as you push it open and step through into your memories . . .

- "Where do you find yourself? . . . What is around you now? . . . Are you inside or outside?. . .

- "Feel your feet and know what you are standing on . . . Is it soft or hard? . . .

- "Get a sense of where you are . . . If you can see clearly, what do you see? . . .

- "Describe it to me, if you can sense where you are; describe that place to me . . .

- "Look at your feet now . . . What color are they? . . . What are you wearing on your feet? . . .

- "Look at the rest of your clothes or get a sense of the clothes you are wearing . . . Tell me what you are called . . . and who is around you . . .

- "Do you get a sense of where this place is? . . . . Is it in Europe, Asia, or America, or some other place? . . . .

- "Do you get a sense of the year you are now remembering? . . ."Have a look around you now . . . Describe to me the people you see around you . . . What are they doing? . . .

- "Have a sense now of the kind of work you do in this life . . . whether you are male or female . . . whether you have friends or family around you and who they are . . .

- "What type of place do you live in? . . . Where do you sleep? . . . Have a sense now of your emotions in this life . . .Tell me about them now. . .

- "Now let those memories start to fade . . . Let those memories start to fade as you step back through the door and you find yourself once more in the time tunnel . . .

- "Find yourself once more in the time tunnel . . . and close that door firmly behind you . . . Close the door behind you . . .

- "Once more, you can feel the sand underneath your feet as you retrace your steps back to the beach . . .

- "Find yourself once more on the lower part of the beach . . . and retrace your footsteps until you reach the stone steps where you entered this part of the beach . . .

- "Step onto the bottom step now . . . that's ten . . . and step up again . . . nine . . . going higher now . . . eight . . . higher and higher. . . seven . . . becoming lighter with each step up . . . six . . . and lighter still. . . five . . . leaving those memories behind you . . . four. . . drifting higher and higher . . . three . . . becoming more aware . . . two . . . and back now onto the first step . . . one . . .

- "You find yourself back at that wooden gate, which opens magically for you, letting you past and allowing you once more to walk on that higher part of the beach . . .

- "Again you retrace your steps, back to where you were first sitting . . . And once more you sit down and you watch the waves . . . and still you are aware of your breathing . . . gentle, steady, rhythmic breaths . . . and you are still feeling warm, comfortable, and relaxed . . .

- "You start to become aware of your physical body once more, sitting in your chair or lying down . . . Become aware of your arms and hands, and move your fingers and then your toes . . .

- "Move your shoulders and your neck, and when you are ready, take a deep breath and open your eyes . . .

- "Welcome back."

• • •

In addition to any notes that your therapist made, you can make some of your own while the experience is fresh in your mind. You may want to ask yourself now whether you recognized anyone who was in that past life with you, as we often collect people around us who travel with us from lifetime to lifetime. We call these souls our soul. Don't worry if you don't recognize anyone; it doesn't always happen.

Health and Reincarnation

9

For some people, health issues stem from a past life. For instance, imagine surviving a fire in which others died, and at the same time having one's lungs damaged by smoke inhalation. The combination of physical and emotional shock in that lifetime can be brought forward into this life, resulting in asthma or other bronchial conditions. Where fears, phobias, or health issues are involved, it is important to receive the right kind of healing to help alleviate these problems. For some people, simply encountering the previous incarnation is a healing experience in itself, but others may need some kind of therapy to help them recover.

Sharon's Asthma

In this lifetime, Sharon suffered from asthma quite badly since she was fourteen, and interestingly it got worse when she came for a regression, so one day, we decided to concentrate on this and see where it went.

The Regression

In a previous life, Sharon discovered that she was a young woman living in the Rockies in Canada. She lived just inside the tree line in a wooden cabin with her cousin and her two children, who were the same souls as her own children in this lifetime. Sharon's husband had died in an accident at work, but she had other relatives living nearby.

One morning, while Sharon's children and cousin were still asleep, she went to the stream to get some fresh water. In the regression session, Sharon could taste the coldness of the water in her mouth, so clearly she must have taken a drink. Sharon was wearing a long floral dress that was tied at the wrists. She also wore boots. She walked along the bank of the stream to a place where the bank was a bit lower, but as she turned around for a moment, she stumbled and fell.

It turned out that trappers had been out during the night before creating a trap for the bears, because they knew that the bears also came to this place to drink. The local bears weren't afraid of human smells because they were used to them, but the

trappers had cut away a part of the bank and had created a trap with stakes that were sticking out at angles to impale the bears. Sharon had fallen onto one of these stakes, which had pierced her chest, causing a fast and fatal bleed. The bears heard her distress call before her family woke up, and a big brown bear tried to hold her chest together while crying out to try to get the attention of her family, which was still inside the cabin. So there was Sharon, with a big brown bear's claws on her chest, knowing that she was dying. The pain was excruciating, and Sharon struggled for breath. As Sharon left that life, she was aware that her children had heard the cry of the bear. They, along with Sharon's cousin, ran to her and tried to save her, but it was impossible.

Sharon knew that her cousin could look after her children, but she was dreadfully distressed at leaving them so young. The grief she felt at the loss of her children in that lifetime was so immense that as she came out of that session, the tears were pouring down her cheeks.

Remembering that past life not only helped Sharon understand why she had always been so protective of her children in this life but also helped her gain more control over her asthma by becoming less stressed.

Krys's Bad Back

Krys has struggled with a back that goes into spasm and out of place since she was in her early twenties. Doctors discovered that three of her lumbar vertebrae (in the lower spine) weren't properly formed at birth. When she was only in her early thirties, doctors told Krys that she would be in a wheelchair within three years. Fortunately, Krys has never had to resort to using a wheelchair; when our regression-therapist friend Moira focused on Krys, this is what she found.

The Regression

Krys was a male Portuguese sailor, and his ship was becalmed in hot weather. Now Krys will tell her story in her own words.

"The year was around AD 1670, and the ship had been becalmed for days on end. We all smelled bad; I was aware that I had lice and that my clothes were filthy. I was wearing trousers that came halfway down my shins, I was barefoot, and I had some sort of a tunic shirt on. There was no food and very little water, and we were all struggling to survive.

"Toward the end of that day, the captain noticed some clouds in the far distance, and in the hope that some wind was due, some of us were sent to climb up the top of the mainsail in order to lower that sail when the wind came. The wind took far longer to arrive than expected, and the captain in his impatience would not allow us back on deck, so we waited and waited in the rigging for the wind to arrive. When it did so, hours later, in my haste to follow orders, I caught my foot in the rigging and fell to the deck below. I survived the fall but broke my back in the process, in exactly the same place where in this life my back is badly formed. I was taken back to Portugal to a sailor's

mission on the point at Cape Saint Vincent. I lived at this small hostel for two or three years, unable to walk or move my feet. I was strapped into an upright chair, and I just sat looking out over my beloved sea. I eventually died from pneumonia."

The Aftermath

Two things followed from this recollection. The first was that Krys's back became considerably better, but it also took kinesiology to make a real improvement, and although Krys's back still aches from time to time, there's no comparison with the way that it was before. However, the second point is really amazing!

Krys always wanted to go to Portugal, and she managed to do so some years later. She went to the Algarve in Portugal on vacation and stayed in a nice city called Lagos. She felt at home there, even though she doesn't speak a word of Portuguese. By chance, during that holiday she visited the Henry the Navigator School in the village of Sagres. The place immediately felt familiar, and though much of it has changed over the years, some parts of it remained the same as they had been in 1670, and she commented that even the sky itself was familiar!

Later that day, Krys traveled a few miles along to Cape Saint Vincent, which is known as "the end of the world" because there is no more land visible from there. On reaching Cape Saint Vincent, she parked her rental car and walked along the roadway. She had an increasing sense of familiarity but also feelings of dread. As she drew closer to the end of the land, she became increasingly uncomfortable. Then Krys reached a place right at the end of the land that had been a hospital many years ago. She realized that she was standing in the very spot where she had died all those centuries ago!

Spontaneous Recall 10

Sometimes a spontaneous past-life memory can be triggered by an object or by visiting a place that you have been to in a previous life. Our friend Imogene had a spontaneous regression that was triggered by an object, and she was able to obtain at least some proof of the story some weeks later.

Imogene tells her story in her own words.

Imogen and the Museum

"One very cold January day about twenty-five years ago, a colleague and I went to Bristol, in southwest England, on business, and we found ourselves with a few hours to kill. We had an early lunch and then decided to take a walk, but a bitter wind blew up and it started to snow, so when we saw a small museum that was open, we went inside. The place appeared to be empty, so my colleague

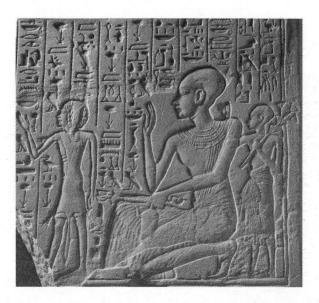

wandered off to look at something that caught his eye. I stood in front of a display of ancient Egyptian artifacts, and I soon found myself looking at a stela. A stela is a tablet with Egyptian writing on it. Sometimes the writing was literally the week's news, and the finished stela would be propped up against the wall of a temple or another important building, where everybody could read it.

"The room started to whirl, and then it disappeared altogether, and a moment later, I was standing in front of a long trestle table that was pushed up against a wall. Set into the wall was a large window. There was no glass in the window, but there were wooden shutters that had been pushed back. The weather was hot, but I was comfortably dressed in a short linen tunic, held together with a loosely fastened brown leather belt. I wore comfortable leather sandals on my feet. I was a slim young man with dark brown, slightly wavy hair that hung down around my neck. There was a woven cane crib on the floor next to the wall behind me, and a baby slept peacefully in it. I knew that this was my baby. I also knew that I was happily married, and that my wife was out shopping for food. This felt like a comfortable, upwardly mobile life.

"On the table in front of me were about a half dozen large, shallow wooden trays. Each tray was about a yard long and about half a yard wide, with raised sides that were about two inches deep. A couple of the trays were empty, while four contained a mixture of mud and some kind of plaster that was in various stages of drying out. At that moment, a girl and boy of about twelve years old came in through an open doorway behind me. I felt that the children were employees or even serfs rather than relatives.

"The children each held the handle of a large, round, cane basket that was lined with large palm leaves. The basket contained the mud-and-plaster mixture. I told them to hurry up because I needed the stuff quickly, and then all three of us lifted the basket and poured its contents into the two empty trays. As I started to spread the mud out with a small wooden trowel, I told the youngsters to go into the living part of the house and get themselves a drink.

"In addition to the trowel, there was a toolbox on the bench. It had staggered levels on both sides and a large handle in the middle. Other than the fact that it was made of wood, it looked exactly like a modern toolbox. The levels contained wooden dies or stamps, which had a variety of marks and images on their undersides. The largest had shapes projecting directly out from the wood, while the medium-size and smaller ones had ends covered in metal, bone, or ivory, with images standing out on them.

"I tested the dryness of a couple of the contents of the trays with my thumb and decided that two were ready, so I moved the toolbox nearer to them. I picked up a sheet of wood that had some notes painted on it. With the sheet in my left hand, I used my right hand to select a number of the stamps, and I started to 'word process' the mixture in the trays. The interesting thing was the speed at which I did the job. Many of the stamps contained whole words or ideas, while some contained letters that made up words, so my 'typing speeds' were not much less than those of many a modern keyboard user! In no time at all, I had filled each stela. I knew that later on, a couple of delivery people would come around and take the dried stelae out of their trays and then cart them out to their appointed destination. These stelae were indeed the newspapers of their day! Soon after this, I heard my business colleague calling me, and I suddenly found myself back in the present time, staring at the stela and feeling rather dizzy.

"When I thought about where and when this might have happened, I felt that it was Thebes, Egypt, in around 2400 BC, and just around the corner from the temple of Karnak. I've never been there in this lifetime, but I know that if I did go, I would be able to find my way from the temple to my old home and office without any difficulty."

The Aftermath

"Some time later I went to central London on business, and this time I tacked on a trip to the British Museum. I went directly to the amazing Egyptian rooms, and unlike all the other tourists, I didn't bother with the mummies but looked around for a stela. I found one in a side cabinet. Interestingly, I could see the wooden trowel and a couple of the stamps from the toolbox on the glass floor of the cabinet. The trowel lay on its side, and I couldn't see the bottom of the stamps. The display case projected from the wall with enough space under it for me to wriggle underneath and look up through the glass. I was just checking out the trowel handle and the metal and ivory ends of the stamps, with their very familiar images on them, when a museum curator came along and asked me what I was doing.

"I scrambled out and told him my story. He then looked at the trowel and stamps (without crawling under the display case) and to my utter astonishment, he said, 'Of course they're yours. Look at the size of your hands and the size of that trowel.'"

Karma and Reincarnation

11

Karma is a way of helping our souls develop over many lifetimes, and it may be viewed in one of two slightly different ways. First, some people see it as a personal score sheet, keeping a tally of their good and bad deeds. So if you were bad in a previous incarnation, you build up karmic debt that somehow needs to be repaid in another incarnation. If you are good in one lifetime, then you add credit to your karmic score sheet, and that offsets previous debts or gives you credits toward a future incarnation. When people talk about karma, they often overlook the credit side and emphasize the karmic-debt aspect. This leads to a view of "what comes around goes around," suggesting a need to experience a bad time in this or some future lifetime in order to repay previous debts.

A much better idea, and the second way karma is conceived, is to consider the way in which our souls develop. Now we look at

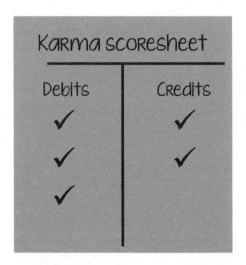

karma from the perspective that each of our souls is on a journey, in which the aim is to develop good qualities and to rid our souls of negative ones. In this approach, there is no score sheet, as the emphasis is on giving your soul the necessary incarnations and experiences that it needs in order to understand what is good and what is bad. Let us illustrate how this may work and the different slant that these two perspectives would have on a particular situation.

Imagine you had a previous incarnation in which you were rich and powerful, but you used this wealth and power to benefit yourself and your favorite people, treating those whom you had power over cruelly, causing them unnecessarily hard lives. In the score-sheet approach, you incurred karmic debt in that incarnation, while in the development approach, you had been given an opportunity to learn how to use wealth and power wisely, but you failed to learn the lesson that time around.

In the score-sheet approach it would now be necessary for you to balance that karmic debt by living an incarnation in which you were subjected to the cruelty and meanness of someone else. The "what comes around goes around" theory is fulfilled, as you have now both been cruel to others and suffered at the hands of someone who is cruel to you. There is no guarantee that this later incarnation will have made your soul wiser; the result may be resentment toward those who hurt you. The soul-development approach determines that your soul still needs to learn the lesson about the wise use of power and wealth, and you will be given more opportunities to do this. Once your soul has grasped this lesson, it will once again be given the opportunity to use a

Soul on a journey

position of power wisely. These kinds of incarnations and life experiences might be repeated until your soul gets the message.

However you choose to view karma, whether it is as a score sheet to be balanced or as soul lessons to be learned, your actions and behavior in previous incarnations can have a massive impact on your present life. It is crucial that you take responsibility for your actions and behavior to others.

It is also of prime importance that you take account of your own soul development. Make sure that you make good use of all the opportunities presented to you in this lifetime to develop good qualities and to learn to trust your own sense of right and wrong.

Many people struggle with the issue of how much they should put themselves first and how much should they be working for the greater good of others. This scenario can be on a small, personal scale, such as when one wonders whether one should put the needs of a partner before one's own. Alternatively, it can be on a global scale, such as when one wonders whether one should give up a lucrative job to go and work for a charity organization in a disaster zone. Each lifetime will present you with a variety of opportunities for getting the balance right.

From our experience, we have seen that it is vitally important that you be true to yourself. Only then can you be a vibrant, well-balanced individual who can genuinely give unconditional love and support to others and behave with integrity. If you get the balance wrong and give, give, give to others without taking care of your own needs, you will not be able to sustain this pattern for long, and you will become worn-out or bitter and resentful. Do things that feel comfortable and right for you, and do the things that make your soul sing—for example, taking the time to express the creative side of your character—and you will have loads more positive energy to give to others. If you overdo things by putting yourself first all the time, however, you will become selfish and uncaring toward others. The trick is to learn this fine balance!

Others
in Our
Incarnations

12

M any of us travel in soul groups in each incarnation, which means that we attract people into our lives who may also have been with us in previous lives. Have you ever met someone new and instantly felt as though you know him or her? You feel a sudden connection to this person, and you sense that you were destined to meet. We have discovered by channeled discussions with those who are now in the discarnate realm and from individuals we have met that we are given signposts along our life's path to help us on our way, and some of these signposts are the people whom we attract into our lives.

Relationships

Now, it may seem to you that if you feel an instant attraction to someone, that person must be very significant in this life, and many of us would see this person as a potential partner, owing to the instant feeling of connectedness that we have. This is great as long as that person is the right partner for you in this life, but sometimes the person is destined to become your great friend rather than your lover. In other cases, it may be that one of your children feels especially connected to you. You don't necessarily love them more than you do your other children, but you feel really connected to them in a way you don't with your other children. You may have feelings of possessiveness toward this child, to the point that you do not want him or her to leave home or marry. As an example, here is the story of a woman we will call Josie:

Josie was suffering because she felt rejected by her son Tim. Because of her great love for Tim, Josie had worked hard to

accept his girlfriend, Polly, into the family, and after a while, Josie had grown to love Polly as well. Everything moved along just fine while Tim and Polly were boyfriend and girlfriend, and even after they announced their engagement, although Josie would often feel upset when Tim and Polly went away together on vacation.

As it happened, Josie also had two other children, and both were in long-term relationships. Her daughter was married with children, and her other son lived away from home. She had never had these feelings of being left out with either of them in the way that she did with Tim. When Tim got married, she was obviously pleased for him because she loves him, but she could not help feeling pushed out of his life. She knew that her feelings didn't make any sense, but she couldn't stop them. Eventually Tim and Polly had children, but puzzlingly, Josie felt as though he should bring them to her instead of having them live with Polly. She began to feel tension building between her daughter-in-law and herself, which then spilled over into her relationship with her son and his children.

When she came to see me, it was clear she had a lot on her mind. During the reading, I began to get a sense that she felt torn by her emotions. When I spoke to her about this battle with her daughter-in-law, she was clearly upset about the situation and couldn't understand why she was affected in this way, especially as this happened only with Tim and his wife and not with her other children. When I spoke to her guides, they started to show me images, thoughts, and feelings from an earlier life. I checked with Josie that she was happy with the idea of reincarnation, and she replied that she was and that she actually felt that she had lived before. Soon I began to unravel the story of her previous life with Tim.

It became apparent that she and Tim had been lovers in a previous life, but because Josie had been from a well-to-do family and Tim had come from a very poor family, they were not allowed to be together in public, although they managed to spend time together whenever they could. Josie's parents in that previous lifetime became aware of her connection to Tim and sent her away to a relative's house. However, she managed to get a message to Tim, and he relocated to be near her. In that lifetime, she was forcibly moved three times, and three times Tim had moved to be near her. However, each time they got together, her parents would find out and move her again.

Finally, Josie's parents forced her to marry someone "suitable," and they found a way to make Tim believe that she really loved the man to whom she was married. Tim went away to war believing that Josie didn't love him any more, and sadly, he lost his life in battle. Josie pined for Tim, not knowing what had happened to her true love, carrying on for a while longer in her loveless marriage until she died in childbirth—presumably being glad to be reunited with Tim in death.

When I spoke to Josie of this, it made perfect sense of her feelings toward her son in this life. She had always felt very, very protective of him and very responsible for him. She had never been able to bear him being out of her sight, and she worried about him all the time whenever he was out of view. This isn't surprising, given that when Tim was out of Josie's sight in the previous lifetime, he lost his life in a war. As her feelings began to make sense to her, Josie began to put them into perspective. No wonder she felt jealous of Polly, because she felt so connected to Tim. Being able to realize that she had shared a life with him previously in such an intense way made her able to relax about him and stop being afraid that something was going to happen to him while he was away from her.

When I saw Josie again some months later, she was much happier. Her relationship with Tim and his wife was fine, and she was enjoying spending time with her grandchildren. Although she did remain slightly more concerned about him than about her other children, she was aware of the origins of her feelings and she was continuing to work on them.

Soul Groups

It has been an endless source of fascination for us to see how souls travel in groups. From our own knowledge, learning, and experience as well as our research, we have found that our soul groups usually consist of twelve souls, but we also interact with other nearby soul groups, which means that we are not limited to close interaction with only twelve souls in each lifetime. Not all souls in the same soul group incarnate in the same lifetime, but even if they do, some of them may incarnate for only a very short

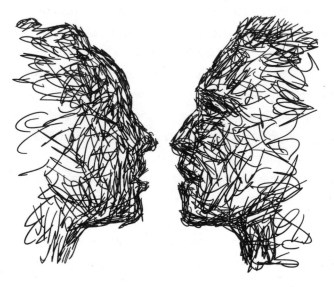

time. We are happy to say that we are in very close contact with most of our soul-group members in this lifetime, and that means that we are surrounded and supported by the love from these close souls. We do hope that you can find these souls in your own lives.

The one you fall in love with may be a member of your soul group or someone from a nearby soul group, and may be someone with whom you have had a very close relationship in a previous life, which is why you feel the instant attraction in this lifetime. Sometimes, though, because we all have free will, we make mistakes in our choice of mate, but when we do this, we can learn something in this lifetime.

Soul-group members are usually family or close friends, so it would be quite unusual if you were to recognize as a member of your soul group someone with whom you have little or no contact. Soul-group members can agree before incarnating that they will come into this life with you in order to help you learn something in particular, but it is unheard of for them to agree to help you by being violent or abusive to you. Our learning on a soul level is with love and nurturing rather than with aggression or anger, no matter what the lesson is. You are most likely to find your soul-group members when you access past-life memories, as they will be the souls whom you recognize as having been close to you in the previous lifetime, and who are close to you again in this lifetime.

You can also find the members of your soul group or members of nearby soul groups in other ways. For example, you may meet someone for the first time and instantly feel that you know him or her in a very clear and deep way, even though you know nothing about this person. This will happen more frequently when you are on your true life's path. Sometimes these people are around you for a short period, perhaps while you are working on a specific project. If you feel deeply about someone, that feeling will be reciprocated if the person is part of your soul group or a nearby one, but if you become obsessed with someone who doesn't return your feelings, something is wrong. In this case, it would be useful for you to explore your feelings with a therapist, because there might be some other spiritual reason that is driving you.

A friend of ours was in a difficult marriage that was getting worse all the time, and then she suddenly fell very heavily for a man who, even by her own admission, was a waste of space. He took her money, made use of her, and then dropped her, but still she obsessed over him, and she couldn't understand why. Eventually, a psychic told her that until this had happened, she couldn't have considered leaving her demanding and unloving husband, but she could now see herself leaving, even though this was not the right man or the right reason. It was as though the idea was a seed that fate had planted in fertile soil, and now it could start to grow.

Eventually, the time would be right and she would leave on her own terms. The medium also told her that she could "see" two wedding rings, meaning that our friend would find a new partner. A few months later, she started to move her goods out of her marital home, and while she was doing so, she met a nice man who was free to be with her.

Gerry and Zena

Here is a much more typical soul group story than the previous one, as this is a story of love.

Zena had been through some hard times, and she endured and survived them, but her life was somewhat arid. It lacked a spiritual center, any real purpose. Zena was divorced and had two adult children who had left home to make their own way in life. She had a lover of sorts, but he was just taking advantage of Zena and keeping her going with promises of a future. The lover was actually in another relationship, and eventually Zena accepted that their relationship had no future. She had a good job in an office and a tiny apartment, so she wasn't unhappy, but she wasn't happy either. She was also lonely and unfulfilled.

Zena had always been interested in spiritual matters, so she studied to be a medium, while also studying tarot, spell casting, and many other similar areas of interest. She had vacation time coming to her from her work and she had a little spare money put away, so when she saw an advertisement for a weeklong residential event that included talks and an opportunity for spiritual readings, Zena signed up for it. She didn't mind going on her own, because she knew that spiritual people tended to be friendly.

At the very first meal, she met Gerry. He was never going to be a romantic attachment, because he was much more like a grandfather figure than any kind of lover. Nevertheless the two of them hit it off from the start, sharing a sense of humor and an uncanny feeling of attachment. They had a lovely week together, and talked for hours about spiritual matters, with the extremely knowledgeable Gerry happily teaching Zena all he could. Over the next few years, Gerry taught Zena even more about spiritual matters, and she showed him the first real affection he had ever had in his long life. Eventually Gerry died. Zena still misses Gerry, but she is grateful to have known him. She learned so much from him, and she gladly enjoyed Gerry's unconditional love. This was a true meeting of souls.

Guides

Many people believe they have a single spirit guide to help them in their lives, but our knowledge and experience shows that we all have many guides and helpers who try to guide us in our earthly lives. We have discovered that these guides are usually souls who have not incarnated in a person's current lifetime but may well have incarnated with that person in previous lifetimes. Helpers may be loved ones, friends, or relatives who have passed to the world of spirit but who still keep an eye on the person from the spirit world. In the rest of this chapter, when we talk about guides, we are including helpers.

Guides and helpers may stay with you for a specific reason, for a season, or indeed for a lifetime. Just as some friends stay with you for life, so some guides stay with you from the moment you are born into this lifetime until you pass on once again. However, there are also guides who are with you for the short term and for a specific reason. For instance, they will come to your aid when you study for exams, if you need to go into the hospital for an operation, or if you are bereaved. These souls become friends to you for the short term, because the spirits are able to empathize with you at that time.

There are guides who can support you and care for you and guides who can help you be in the right place at the right time. You have probably had intense but short-term friendships for a short time, like the inseparable school friend with whom you have long since lost touch. In the same way, you have guides who are with you for a season. You may have a guide who looks after you during your growing years, or when you are going through your child-rearing years (we certainly need help then) or your older years. As you move on from those phases, you no longer need the expertise of some guides; you move on to other guides who are more suitable in the new situation. In this way, you have some guides and helpers for life and others who come and go.

We, the authors, know this from our personal experiences, and from the times that we have spent looking into the discarnate realm, where we have met and had discussions with our guides. We have recalled conversations with them, when they have helped us choose which lifetime and which experiences we should encounter the next time around.

Some individuals we know find it useful to be regressed so that they return to the discarnate realm and speak to their guides, especially if a difficult or challenging past life has just been revealed to them. From guided visualizations in which we have helped people connect with their guides and helpers, it has often been reported that they feel an amazingly powerful and unconditional level of love and support from their guides. In this way, they gain help, support, and guidance during times of difficulty.

Your guides and helpers always want what is best for you; they will help point you in the quickest or best direction when you are facing choices or challenges in your life, but remember that you always have free will to act as you choose. Your guides will never abandon you because of something that you choose to do or something you avoid doing, but a good, strong connection with your guides can help you see your options clearly and gauge your best way forward.

Samantha's Guide

Our friend Samantha told us this dramatic story about how she received help from a short-term guide. Samantha spent several years in Johannesburg, South Africa, and while she was there, she took a course on the Kabbala. This involved several meditation sessions, one of which was designed to introduce the students to their guide or guides. Samantha had always felt protected in Africa, even in the most dangerous situations, and during one of these meditation sessions, she discovered why.

Apart from the occasional dangers of living in Johannesburg, Samantha had spent time in the bush, and while she was there, she had gone on a walking tour with a small group, led by a ranger, complete with his rifle. The ranger looked for all the world like a less-than-handsome Indiana Jones, floppy hat and all. Samantha tried to keep up with the group, but being smaller than the others and not particularly strong, she soon fell behind. As she was wandering along, looking with fascination at the unfamiliar landscape, she noticed a large, spotted catlike animal quietly trotting along, about six feet off to her right, just on the other side of a line of shrubs. Samantha has always been fond of animals, and they instinctively relax and trust her, so she wasn't surprised when the "cat" ambled alongside, keeping her company for a while. Then it turned toward her and smiled at her (Samantha swears this is true) before turning away and ambling off into the bush. A little while later, Samantha caught up with the group.

When she told them of her experience, the ranger jumped up in a panic. When she described the animal, he blanched and said it was a leopard. He then raised his rifle and looked around frantically. Samantha was horrified at the idea that the ranger might shoot her leopard, so she inwardly begged the creature to move away quickly if it was still around. She said that at no moment had she felt even the tiniest bit afraid of the leopard.

The meditation sessions showed Samantha that she had a guide called Omar Pilli, who had lived in Africa many centuries before Europeans arrived. Omar Pilli was a tall, well-built, courageous hunter and warrior, and he knew the bush and its wildlife very well. She was sure that Omar Pilli had protected both her and the leopard by quietly leading it out of harm's way. After Samantha returned to the United Kingdom, Omar Pilli disappeared from her orbit, but she is confident that if she ever found herself back in the wilderness, her trusty African guide would immediately come to her aid.

The
Discarnate
Realm

13

So, what is the discarnate realm? Some people call it "the life between lives," while others call it Heaven, the universe, the Great Spirit, or the Source. You must call it whatever feels comfortable to you. We, the authors, like to refer to this place as the discarnate realm, which means the place where your soul exists without an incarnate form. Our experience of regression for ourselves and for others has been that the discarnate realm is a place of love and joy, healing and learning. It is not a place of helplessness or hopelessness, nor is it a place of retribution or punishment.

This can be a difficult concept, especially for humans who in this lifetime have suffered at the hands of others or who have seen loved ones mistreated. It is our belief that we heal and learn in the discarnate realm. We also believe that there is no such thing as an evil soul, although there are humans who commit evil acts and behave in bad ways.

So, what happens with those souls when they pass to spirit? They will learn from their errors, and they will be guided and supported just as we all are. They may choose to reincarnate to a life where they learn the human experience of suffering in their turn, or they may choose to reincarnate to a life where they have the same opportunities and choices and this time use their power only for good. It is worth repeating that we all have free will during our human lives, and this means that the choices we make affect us in some way, just as the choices of our parents and others around us can also affect us.

We also have a further belief. We consider that the soul still exists in the discarnate realm even when we are incarnating in human form, and we call this our higher self. Imagine that your soul is a ball of light, and when you reincarnate, a sliver of that light travels down and becomes a human existence. However, the main ball of light remains in the discarnate realm, so the larger part of your soul remains there. For us, this explains several difficult concepts. We do not want to confuse you with these concepts or force our beliefs on you; all we can tell you is that these ideas have come from the knowledge, experience, and reading we have done.

Déjà Vu

One form of déjà vu occurs when you go somewhere that is new to you and feel that you have been there before. This may be due to a triggering of your memory of a previous incarnation. Another type of déjà vu occurs when you are talking with someone and you feel that you have had the exact same conversation before, with the exact same person, and that you are standing in exactly the same place. In this case, you know exactly what is going to be said and done next. We believe this is because your soul in the discarnate realm knows what is going to happen and what will be said a split second before your conscious mind does. This feeds back to your human mind to cause the déjà vu experience.

Your Higher Self

Sometimes, during a guided visualization, you will be able to connect with your higher self to work out your best route forward in life or the way out of a difficult situation. Sometimes this happens during sleep, and you wake up with the answer.

Greeting Someone In the Discarnate Realm while You Are Still Alive

This again comes from our past-life experiences, when we have gone through the death experience in a past-life memory and met loved ones who were actually still incarnating in human form at the time of that past-life death. Once again, this is because the main part of our soul is always in the discarnate realm, so when we pass over, the first reassurance that we need is a familiar energy around us, and who best to show us that but our loved ones, whether they have actually passed over or are still living in human form.

This also explains how those who have passed to spirit can still communicate with us from the spirit world via mediums, even after they have incarnated into another human form. The largest part of our soul is always in the discarnate realm, so all our human experiences and memories are available to our loved ones who

remain behind in earthly form. Some spiritualists do not believe in reincarnation because they believe that when a soul incarnates again, it is no longer able to communicate from spirit. We hope this explains how that soul still can communicate, even if the person is back on earth in another lifetime.

We know the discarnate realm to be filled with love, goodness, and healing, where all souls grow and develop. It is a place of learning and peace, and it is filled with joy and happiness. Those souls who have been parted in life are overjoyed to meet again in the discarnate realm.

Some people believe that the discarnate realm contains certain levels and that some souls are not allowed to reach some of these levels until they progress. We do not hold this belief system. We believe that all souls may experience all parts of this realm, and that restricted access to different levels is a wholly human belief that doesn't have any bearing in reality.

Soul Names

We have discovered that every one of us has a soul name. This name transcends all our physical lifetimes, and our soul uses it between physical lives, so this one eternal soul name stays with our soul across all time. In the discarnate realm, it is possible to access your soul name. If you are in a regression or a guided visualization, then you may know, hear, or see your own soul name for yourself. If you are in a therapy session such as recession, or having a reading, then the therapist or reader may access this information for you and tell it to you, but it's always better for you

to get this particular piece of information for yourself, if possible. It may be that your soul name does not translate into your current native language or into any language spoken today. If this is the case, you will receive an approximation of the sound of your name.

When you discover your soul name, you are likely to feel very excited, and we recommend that you take some time to get used to thinking of yourself as this name, maybe saying the name aloud or writing it down. Take time to get a sense of how this eternal name feels to you. Once you know your soul name, you may see this name in unusual places. We used to walk past an advertisement without really looking at it, and then after learning our soul names, the letters that spelled our names jumped out at us from the wall! We recommend that you become familiar with your soul name yourself before deciding whether you want to share this information with anyone else. We are not saying that you should not share it, but do not do so in haste when you are excited!

The soul name for each person is special to that soul, so we advise you not to access the soul name of someone else, although there are exceptions to this rule, for instance, when an individual asks a reader or therapist to perform this service. If you and your good friend or companion feel closely connected across a number of lifetimes (and if the other person agrees) you can locate your friend's soul name.

Knowing your own soul name can be incredibly empowering. You can use this eternal name for yourself in meditation, in positive affirmations, in therapy sessions, and during past-life work. You may even find that this name is present in your dreams.

Your True Path

There are times when the recalling of a particular incarnation will have a profound impact on the whole future direction of your life. This is exactly what happened to Elaine, as it resulted in a total change of direction. On entering that past lifetime, Elaine found herself to be a young boy playing in the ashes of a fire, along with her older sister. Neither of their names translated into English, so for the sake of simplicity Elaine called the boy Ho and his sister Lin.

While Ho was messing around at the edge of the fire, making patterns on his hands with the ash, his older sister, Lin, was learning to write ancient symbols with her finger in the cool ash at the edge of the fire. These special symbols represented the herbs and remedies that they would both later learn to prepare when they became healers, because Ho discovered that he and Lin were being trained by their mother and another woman to become healers.

Ho and Lin would accompany their mother and the other healer on journeys away from their camp, traveling into the foothills of the great mountain nearby. Each journey was carefully timed to gather herbs, spices, and roots at the best possible time. On returning to the camp, they would prepare these materials in the correct way for each item, so some were dried above the fire, while others were chopped or crushed. Each was kept in the right box with the correct symbol on the lid. As Ho moved on in that lifetime, he and Lin spent most of their time carefully watching their mother and the other healer of the tribe, learning how to combine different ingredients into a variety of healing remedies and to know which remedies were used for each illness or injury. Elaine felt that this lifetime was around 3000 BC. The first scenes that she recalled seemed to be located in the foothills of a great mountain, but the tribe moved between two locations depending on the season, and the second location was in a wide valley near a big river.

After recalling this past life, Elaine felt a real need to change direction, and she has subsequently trained as a complementary health practitioner.

Past and Present

14

Let us look at a few of the questions that we all ask ourselves from time to time about the way that previous lives might affect our present ones, if they do at all.

Past Joys and Present Woes

Is everything that goes wrong in your current life caused by something that happened in a previous one? Probably not. You may have had dozens of past lives, and it would take many sessions to uncover all the reasons for your current problems, if that were even possible. Most past lives are quite ordinary, so probably only those ones that have some special importance or a direct bearing on the present will surface in your regression or recession sessions. Some past-life events might explain something about your present circumstances, but not all will. This life is part of your soul's journey and part of the learning pattern for the future, whether it is to be carried out in a future life or in the discarnate realm.

Charmed Lives Versus Difficult Ones

When you look around, you are bound to see neighbors and acquaintances who seem to have charmed lives. They have the relationships, money, or lifestyle that you lack, and you can't see what they have done to deserve it. Have they perhaps been very good in a past life? Is that it? Maybe so. They might be being given a particularly easy ride this time round, either in payment for past behavior or just as a kind of rest cure.

Is Pain All Due to Past Lives?

In some cases, emotional or physical pain can be traced back to a past life, but sometimes unhappiness is just part of the soul's journey. A perfect life doesn't teach you anything, while times of trouble are both character building and karmically beneficial. You've no doubt seen friends whose life partners have left them or who are let down learn to cope with things that they would never have done otherwise.

We remember one woman whose accountant husband didn't bother to do his own bookkeeping or pay his taxes. Eventually the Inland Revenue caught up with him, and the resultant fines cost the couple their home and their comfortable lifestyle. After this, the husband sat slumped in a chair, defeated and emotionally paralyzed; the hitherto cosseted wife had to take over. She suddenly found herself dealing with lawyers and real estate people, and she even managed to restart her husband's business by talking his clients into remaining with him.

Her husband gradually came out of his slump and took back the reins of his work, but the wife never went back to the homemaker role or relied totally on her husband again. She said that discovering her own inner strength took her by surprise, and from that time on, their marriage was one of equals.

This situation didn't arise from anything that had happened in a past life, but it may have a bearing on her behavior in a future one.

Love and Obsession

Doomed love has kept writers busy for centuries. The most recognizable story is perhaps *Romeo and Juliet*. In our time, the theme of religious embargo is explored in films like *Witness*, which took detective Harrison Ford into the Amish community, and a similar story, *A Stranger Among Us*, where another detective, this time, Melanie Griffith, investigated a death at a Yeshiva and fell in love with an orthodox Jewish man. Even the television program *Moonlight* has at its center the unrequited love of a human woman for a vampire. Today, there is little to stop any of us from living

with whomever we like, and while parents, friends, and even our current partner might object, they can't do much to stop us. But there is, indeed, one thing that does stop us—the lover who refuses to give us what we want.

Psychics are always being asked questions about love, as the path of true love is so often such a stony one. Perhaps the object of desire is made all the more fascinating by being unobtainable.

With unrequited love, it's a fact that you can't always have what you want, however much you yearn for it. Modern self-help books will tell you that "cosmic ordering" and "laws of attraction" can give you everything you want; however, while a positive mental attitude can help in practical matters such as money and work, it rarely helps in the case of unrequited love. You cannot cosmically order someone to give up his or her personal agenda for your sake.

Obesity and Other Problems

There is a theory that if a person overeats it's because he or she starved in a previous life. Regression might uncover the reasons for the overeating, and that knowledge might help the individual deal with the weight problem in this life. Similarly, if someone can't stop spending money on clothes, jewelry, cars, nice bags and belts, and so on, it might be due to too much poverty in the preceding lives. Recession or regression might help you see how a past-life situation is being played out in this one, but if nothing relevant shows up, then the situation may just be a lesson for this life. Ultimately, whatever your problem and whatever its root cause, you will have to deal with the situation in the here and now. Perhaps hypnotherapy can help.

The Golden Rule

Whatever steps you take to improve your own life, you should try to avoid hurting others whenever possible, if for no other reason than to avoid building up bad karma for yourself. It's also worth bearing in mind that allowing others to treat you badly builds up bad karma for them.

We go through many lives and many situations. We enjoy good health in one life and sickness in another; we experience wealth, importance, and power on one occasion, or poverty and bad treatment in another. We have much-loved children or too many unwanted babies. Maybe we can't have a child this time round. We may have loving or unloving parents, harsh bosses or kindly ones, or situations that either free us or trap us. We may have everything that we could desire, and even that could be the result of past actions. Looking back to previous lives might provide some answers.

Conclusion

We hope you go on from here to explore your own past lives in whatever way appeals to you. You may choose to have a past-life reading, but if you feel that you have issues in your life that are rooted in a previous incarnation, we advise that you seek the services of a suitably qualified therapist for hypnosis or regression.

There is one rather mysterious way in which you can find yourself drawn to a particular psychic, kinesiologist, or past- life therapist, which occurs when you happen to hear someone's name from three different sources; when this happens, it means that the universe is trying to draw your attention to that person.

We hope you have enjoyed reading and learning about past lives and that you have enjoyed our experiences and the stories of some individuals we know. We have tried to give you evidence to support our beliefs, and we hope you read this book with an open mind.

We now ask that you please take our best wishes with you.

About the Authors

Krys and Jass Godly are known world-wide as mediums, psychics, therapists, radio show hosts, and authors. They are also practitioners of kinesiology, hypnotherapy, past life regression, reflexology, and reiki. All of these services, except reflexology, are available remotely. To contact them, visit their website at *http://betterhealthchoice.co.uk*

In 2015, they were recipients of the Lightworkers Award, an international award which recognizes excellence in the esoteric arts.

Try another practical guide in the
ORION PLAIN AND SIMPLE
series

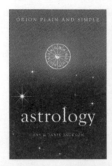

astrology

totem animals

runes

palmistry

body reading

numerology

chinese astrology

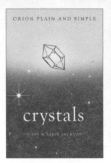

crystals

reincarnation

angels

OG